JAPAN
A Short History

Supervised
by John Gillespie, Ph.D.

ICG Muse, Inc.
New York, Tokyo, Osaka & London

Published by ICG Muse, Inc.
73 Spring Street, #206, New York, NY 10012.
2-7-20 Kita-Aoyama, Minato-ku, Tokyo 107-0061.

Distributed by Tuttle Shokai Inc.
2-7-20 Kita-Aoyama, Minato-ku, Tokyo 107-0061.

ISBN 4-925080-35-0

First edition, 2001.

CONTENTS

ECHIZEN
KAGA
NOTO
SADO
ECHIGO
DEWA   MUTSU
ECCHU
KOZUKE
SHIMOTSUKE
HITACHI
HIDA   SHINANO
MUSASHI
MINO
KAI
SHIMOSA
OMI
OWARI
MIKAWA   SURUGA
KAZUSA
ISE
IZU   AWA
SHIMA
SAGAMI
IGA
YAMATO
TOTOMI
YAMASHIRO

Chapter I: Dawn of the Nation

1. Prehistoric Era

Where do the Japanese come from? It is a common belief in Japan that the Japanese are homogeneous, in part because Japan is surrounded by ocean and hence isolated from the rest of the world. Yet, throughout her history Japan has had many and ongoing interactions and exchanges with the international community.

• *Jomon-style pottery.*

Japan consists of four major islands with almost three thousand smaller ones. It was geographically connected to the Asian continent in prehistoric times (more than fifteen thousand years ago). Indeed, the bones of mammoths and many other animals from other parts of the world have been found in Japan.

It is unknown when Japan was first inhabited, but the most widely accepted hypothesis suggests that people came from southern Asia and the Pacific as well as from the north some twenty thousand years ago.

• *Yayoi-style pottery.*

More than two thousand prehistoric artifacts have been discovered in Japan. Those artifacts increase in number after about 8,000 B.C., the period characterized by primitive villages of hunters and fishermen and made distinctive by clay pots decorated with cord marks. The Japanese word for these cord designs, *jomon*, is also the name of the period itself.

During the Jomon Period, the Japanese gradually imported farming skills from the rest of the Asia. Around this time in China, the Chinese writing system and many other technologies were developed and exported to the other nations and outlying tribes. The

• *Fang-shaped accessories made by jade or agate.*

• Bronze bell used in religious rites.

Japanese "tribe" was no exception, adopting certain aspects of Chinese culture around the third century B.C.

As with the Jomon Period, this next era takes its name—*Yayoi*—from its distinctive pottery and clay figures. Important developments of this era include the implementation of Chinese agricultural techniques such as irrigated rice fields and the widespread use of wooden, bronze, and iron tools.

• Clay figure of a warrior.

2. FORMING THE NATION

Continental Asian influence was pivotal in the political and cultural history of ancient Japan. Actually, it is unclear exactly how the Japanese were united as one nation. Modern Japanese may well be the descendants of continental Asian tribes who came to Japan in successive waves, with relatively sophisticated, Chinese-influenced technologies.

China was united around 221 B.C. with the establishment of the Qin Dynasty and a new imperial government. Around the time of Jesus Christ, China greatly expanded its reach and became somewhat like the Roman Empire. It is quite natural therefore to imagine that there would be many interactions between such an influential center of power and the relatively weaker villages and tribes inhabiting Korea and the Japanese islands.

The Chinese impact stimulated some of those tribes to create more powerful political organizations. The very first recorded visit of a Japanese envoy to the Han court was in A.D. 57, but it probably was not until around the third century A.D. that the first movements toward creating nations began in both the Korean Peninsula and in Japan.

During this time, the mysterious prophetess Himiko was recorded in Chinese historical records as queen of the Yamatai kingdom in Japan. This kingdom is recorded as having had contact with the court of the Wei Dynasty in China. The Japanese are described in these records as being law-abiding people who paid close attention to social hierarchies. They practiced agriculture and fishing, as well as spinning and weaving. The records further note, interestingly, that the rulers of the early Japanese were some-

• *Bronze mirrors.*

• *Reconstruction of a watch-tower at Yoshinogari site, Saga Pref.*

times male and sometimes female.

Still today archeologists argue about where Yamatai's capital was located. Some say it was in Kyushu, while others believe it was in the Yamato area where the imperial government was first established a century later. Drawing historical clues from Shinto legends has suggested that although the original capital may have been in Kyushu, the Yamato clan, growing in power, decided to gradually move north and east toward the area where the first government was eventually formed.

3. YAMATO YEARS

Japan was once a nation where the emperor was regarded as divine. Of course, the current imperial system bears more resemblance to that of the United Kingdom—that is, the emperor is regarded merely as a symbol of the nation and there is no political power belonging to the imperial court.

However, until the end of the Second World War, the situation was different. It is remarkable that the Japanese followed and respected the same imperial tradition from the beginning of their history until 1945. As the principal exemplar of that tradition, the emperor had tremendous influence on Japanese politics and culture.

A strong imperial government was first formed around the end of third century A.D. It is referred to as the Yamato Imperial Court, be-

cause it was located in the region called Yamato, south of Kyoto and extending to the center of the Kii Peninsula. Exactly how such a strong government was created is unclear, but it was apparently forged through an intense power struggle during the latter part of third century.

Interestingly the Yamato power struggle was related to the political movement on the Korean Peninsula. According to Chinese histories of the time, Japanese were asked during the battles among Korean kingdoms to send troops to support Paekche (Kudara in Japanese), the kingdom located in the southwest part of the Korean Peninsula. There was a major battle between Koguryo (Kokuri in Japanese), the kingdom to the north, and Japanese troops in the year of 391 A.D.

Keyhole-shaped burial mound for the Emperor Nintoku.

This event suggests an intriguing possibility—namely, whether the Japanese imperial clan in fact came from the Korean tribes who had invaded Japanese soil in earlier years. If so, it is quite reasonable to conclude that the Japanese emperor sent troops to Korea to protect his interests. Or did the Japanese unite and marshal their own forces with a view to conquering the Korean Peninsula? Many hypotheses are still heard among archeologists, anthropologists, and historians.

Since the end of the fourth century, the Japanese periodically revealed their political and territorial interest in Korea. In 662 A.D., the Chinese navy stifled that interest for a long time by defeating the Japanese navy and supporting Shilla (Shiragi in Japanese,) the kingdom in the western part of the Korean Peninsula.

This series of battles indicates that Japan was deeply involved with the Asian continent from the beginning of its recorded history. Indeed, Japan took its early identity as a nation not from any domestic initiative but from the consciousness of its connection to Korea and even China, which was also interested in hegemony over the Korean Peninsula. In fact, when the Japanese imperial government was formed, thousands of Koreans and Chinese came to Japan and were hired by government and powerful local leaders to contribute to the development of the nation. They brought not only technology but also *Kanji*, or Chinese characters, a sophisticated writing system that the Japanese adopted. Also, many Japanese emperors sent delegations to China to create economic, cultural and political interactions with the Chinese government.

The power of the Yamato government is confirmed in their *kofun*, or burial mounds. Between the third and fifth centuries, the imperial family and strong local leaders created huge *kofun* throughout Japan but particularly in the Yamato region and surrounding areas. The largest *kofun* is the one built for the Emperor Nintoku, created in the fifth century. It is one of the largest tombs in the world, with a distinctive keyhole shape.

From the fifth and into the sixth century, Yamato emperors established their influence over all of Japan except for the northern part of Honshu and Hokkaido, which were considered almost as separate nations with different tribes of people.

4. ARRIVAL OF BUDDHISM

Buddhism entered Japan in the middle of the sixth century, principally through the medium of Chinese and Korean priests. Buddhism was not only religion and philosophy. It was a distinctive, cosmopolitan civilization. The priests, who were the main scholars and intellectuals of the time, brought valuable practical culture, such as medical technology, irrigation and so on, along with their ways of thought.

Buddhist temples are everywhere in Japan today and one might even conclude, wrongly, that Buddhism was an integral part of Japanese culture from the beginning of Japanese recorded history. In fact, Buddhism can stand as the sixth-century symbol of internationalization. After Siddhartha Gautama created this cosmopolitan religion, it took 1,000 years to arrive in Japan. During this lengthy period, Buddhism encountered other cultures and religions. For example, the expedition of Alexander the Great to Central Asia brought Greek culture into contact with Buddhism.

Of course, with its establishment in India, Buddhism had considerable influences from ancient Indian civilization. Many other influences helped shape Buddhism as it gradually moved eastward through China, Southeast Asia, and Korea. Therefore, when Buddhism finally arrived in Japan, it brought not only a distinctive religion but other benefits such as its cosmopolitan world-view.

At the same time, however, Buddhism was so new and different from Japan's indigenous culture that some people were concerned that it might impact Japan as an alien cultural invasion. Indeed, this concern created serious political battles among the powerful clans of the imperial government. This struggle came to the end in 587, when the Soga clan, which supported Buddhism, defeated the Mononobe clan, which was opposed.

During the era of Soga clan's prosperity, Buddhism was widely accepted under the leadership of the Yamato imperial government. Prince Shotoku established his leadership at this time, serving as regent to the Empress Suiko. He also opened an official diplomatic relationship with the Sui Dynasty of China and sent an envoy named Kenzui-shi. This envoy system continued to the beginning of the tenth century, sending hundreds of students to study in China.

• *Image hall of Horyu-ji temple.*

• *Prince Shotoku.*

Prince Shotoku is also known as the creator of Japan's first constitution, with its famous 17 articles. His era is called the Asuka Period, named after the location of their governmental buildings. The Asuka Period is associated with the earliest Buddhist culture found in Japan. For example, Horyu-ji temple was first built during this time and is known as the oldest wooden structure in the world. Its architecture and sculptures reveal extensive international influence.

After the death of Prince Shotoku in 622, a power struggle broke out between the Soga clan and others who coveted power. Eventually, in 645 Prince Nakano-oe (or Nakano-oe no Oji), who was supported by Nakatomi no Kamatari, assassinated Soga no Iruka, head of the Soga clan. This coup d'état launched a complete reformation of the imperial government called *Taika no Kaishin*, or the Taika Reform.

The new government centralized its power on the Chinese model. The main change was to institute effective tax management through the registry system. Prince Nakano-oe became the Emperor Tenchi in 668, and, by the time of his successor, the Emperor Temmu, in 673, he had established a new bureaucracy and legal system.

The imperial government supported as part of its national policy, using Buddhist philosophy and religious power to stabilize the country.

• *Yume-dono, or Hall of Dreams, of Horyu-ji temple.*

Chapter II: Tempyo and Heian

5. TEMPYO PERIOD

When Yakushi-ji temple was built at the end of seventh century, China was under the Tang Dynasty. Tang China was one of the most prosperous empires in world history. Its territory extended to the eastern edges of the Middle East, where exchanges between eastern and western cultures were actively taking place. China's western neighbor at the time was the Saracen Muslim Empire, the impact of which reached western Europe. In fact, China and the Saracens were the world's two leading civilizations where one could find the most advanced technology.

The trade route between China and the Saracens was called the Silk Road, along which countless merchants, monks, students and soldiers traveled. The Silk Road was the path used to introduce sophisticated paper-making technology from China to the West, after the Saracen army defeated the Tang army in 651. Marco Polo traveled along the route

• *Image hall of Todai-ji temple.*

six hundred years later. The Silk Road extended west to Italy and Spain and east to Japan.

Between Prince Shotoku's era and the beginning of the ninth century, Japan absorbed a cosmopolitan civilization from China. Based on that influence, the imperial government established the law called *Taiho Ritsuryo*, or the Taiho Constitution, covering legal matters, tax, social class, the military and the political system.

Therefore, when the Empress Gemmei decided to move her capital to Nara in 710, Japan was already an established nation with a sophisticated government and legal system. When Nara was designed, the Japanese used as their model the street system of Chang'an, the Tang Dynasty capital. This era between 710 and 784, when the Japanese capital was located at Nara, is called the Tempyo Period or the Nara Period.

This was an active era for Japan, the terminal of the Silk Road. Envoys to Tang Dynasty China were periodically dispatched. Many students sent to

• *Model of reconstructed Fujiwara-kyo.*

China played important roles in the imperial government after they returned to Japan. It was also during this period when the first currency was circulated in Japan, based on influence from China.

The Tempyo Period is also known as the era when Buddhism became influential in Japanese politics. For example, the Emperor Shomu thought that if Buddhism

• *Reconstruction of Sujaku-mon gate of Heijo-kyo.*

• *Image hall of Yakushi-ji temple.*

were widely respected, national crises such as rebellions or natural disasters could be prevented. Thus, he ordered a huge statue of Buddha to be built in the capital to symbolize his belief. You can see this statue today in the Todai-ji temple in Nara. Todai-ji is also known for its treasure house, the Shoso-in, with its vast array of musical instruments, pottery, and decorative arts that came from China, India and the Middle East in the Tempyo Period.

Imperial support of Buddhism gave Buddhist monks considerable power, and they started to exert their influence on the central government. This caused some

political turmoil after the Emperor Shomu's death, starting with the negative impact on farmers of the heavy taxes levied to build the Todai-ji.

Tempyo was also the era when Japan's first historical documents, *Kojiki* and *Nihonshoki*, were published. *Kojiki* presents the mythology of ancient Japan, while *Nihonshoki* relates the history of the establishment of the Yamato era. The most notable Tempyo publication was *Man'-yoshu* (the Collection of Myriad Leaves), a poetry anthology compiled between the Yamato and Tempyo periods. The Tempyo era came to an end when the Emperor Kammu decided to move the imperial capital to Nagaoka, in the suburbs of Kyoto, in 784.

• *Cloister of Kasuga Shrine.*

6. Era of Reconciliation between Shintoism and Buddhism

Political struggles caused the new capital in Nagaoka to be abandoned before construction was complete. By 794, the capital was moved to Heian-kyo, now known as Kyoto, and the ensuing era, to 1192, is called the Heian Period. The city of Heian-kyo, like Nara, was also laid out on the model of the Tang Dynasty capital Chang'an. In fact, the early part of the Heian Period was quite similar to Tempyo, when continental

• *Ise Shrine.*

Asian influence was abundant. There were trade relationships with China, Korea and Bohai (Bokkai in Japanese), a kingdom located in Manchuria and eastern Siberia.

At the beginning of the ninth century, the priests Saicho and Kukai returned from China and established, respectively, Tendai-shu and Shingon-shu, esoteric Buddhists sects, destined to become very influential. Their philo-

sophical theories were so complicated that monks were required to study and train for years under ascetic disciplines. Many temples

• *City wall of Xi'an, ancient Chang'an.*

were created in the deep mountain areas for the monks to be isolated from normal life.

Gradually these new Buddhist sects mingled with local Japanese religions and created a unique set of religious practices. Traditionally, Japanese believed that *kami*, or spirits, were inherent in nature. Mountains, waterfalls, lakes, stones and trees were respected as embodying those spirits. This belief developed over time and became ritualized. The practices used to demonstrate this belief became the religion known as *Shinto*, or the Way of the Gods.

Shinto is often seen as the religion of the emperor's family. That is partially true: there are many Shinto shrines deeply related to the imperial family. A typical example is Ise Shrine, established in the early part of the Yamato era. It is also true, however, that every

• *Oratory of Heian Shrine. This was constructed as the reduction of old Heian-kyo's palace, Daigoku-den.*

local region had its own animist belief in the spirits of nature. Eventually, these local regions created Shinto shrines to show respect for their local *kami*. Only in the late nineteenth century, because of the political needs of the new imperial government, was this diversity of local religions officially unified as one Shinto religion.

During the ninth century, the newly established esoteric Buddhist sects, given their remote locations deep in the mountains, began to adopt Shinto practices. For example, Buddhist monks began to show their deep respect for nature by adopting various Shinto practices such as purification rituals. Through this process of mingling and cross-fertilization, Buddhism was finally recognized as the national religion during the Heian Period.

Showing respect by practicing certain rituals or forms has persisted into the life of modern Japan, including the Japanese business world. Evidence of these practices can be seen, for example, in exchanging business cards, having a Shinto priest recite prayers on beginning the construction of a new building, and in the distinctive manner in which the stock exchange is closed at the end of every year. Strictly following such rituals and forms is still considered quite important to business effectiveness in Japan.

• *Mandala.*

17

7. ERA OF THE TALE OF GENJI

The adaptation of Shintoism by Buddhists can be understood as a kind of process of "Japanization" of foreign culture, a trend seen throughout Japan's history. The Heian Period offers an excellent example of that trend. The Tang Dynasty in China was crumbling and finally perished in 907. A period of civil war ensued until the Song Dynasty emerged in 960. This situation gave Japan a chance to digest the foreign culture it had borrowed from China and to accommodate it to her own tradition. This process eventually helped Japan establish her own cultural identity.

For example, the Japanese took Chinese characters, modified and simplified many of them, and created their own writing system—a combination of Chinese characters and the phonetic systems, *hiragana* and *katakana*. With this evolving system of writing, they created a rich array of novels, poems and essays.

Perhaps the best known of these literary works is Lady Murasaki's *Genji Monogatari*, or the Tale of Genji, completed at the beginning of the eleventh century. This great love story is widely recognized as the world's first novel. In fact, the Heian Period was a time of vigorous literary creativity, with some of the best writing by women, who were the daughters, wives and mistresses of aristocrats. The world described in *the Tale of Genji* was the life of the imperial court and aristocrats in it and attendant upon it.

The presiding power in the Heian Period was the Fujiwara clan. They were the descendants of Nakatomi no Kamatari, who

• *The Tale of Genji Scroll.*

had played the pivotal role in *Taika no Kaishin*, or the Taika Reform, in 645. The Fujiwara clan maintained power by two grand strategies—economically, they controlled vast areas of farmland throughout Japan, and politically, they dominated governmental power through a series of political mar-

• *Vehicle for the court nobles.*

riages with the emperor's family. Their extravagant life was so excessive that it eventually created chaos in the imperial government, most notably in the devastation of local areas without regard for proper restraints. Indeed, while the Fujiwara clan enjoyed their prosperity, a new movement was brewing in rural areas.

In both the Tempyo and the early part of the Heian Period, all land belonged to the nation. There was one important exception: rural land that was newly cultivated could be privately owned. Under this exception, the Fujiwara clan and large temples with power and wealth invested their money in cultivating new land in the provinces. Thus, the imperial tax system established with *Taiho Ritsuryo*, or the Taiho Constitution,

gradually collapsed. To protect their land and to receive private taxes from it, the powerful aristocrats and temples hired professional warriors, called *bushi,* or samurai. Around the middle of the tenth century, many of these warriors were aligned with one of the two most powerful clans—Genji and Heike.

In 1086, after the several skirmishes, the Fujiwara clan restored the political power of the imperial court to the imperial family. However, the economic and political situation only became worse, because the emperor—particularly his father Ho'oh—more or less governed by the same means as the Fujiwara clan. In fact, to maintain the safety and stability of their government, they were also dependent on the power of professional warriors. This powerful *bushi,* or samurai, class was gradually transforming the old imperial and aristocratic society.

• *Lady Murasaki.*

Chapter III: Medieval Society

8. Genji and Heike

By the mid-twelfth century, *bushi* had begun to play a major role in Japanese politics. Two rivals, the Genji and Heike clans, fought each other for control of the country between 1159 and 1185. Their struggle is often referred to as the Gempei War, from the first part of each clan's name.

At first, the Heike clan took control under the leadership of Taira no Kiyomori, the Heike leader, but it was later defeated by the Genji clan in an important series of battles. Their struggle was described in the epic literary work *Heike Monogatari*, or the Tale of Heike. Nobody knows who wrote this long story, but its lyrics have been sung by traveling monk singers to the accompaniment of the *biwa*, or Japanese lute.

After the fall of the Heike, the Genji leader, Minamoto no Yoritomo, became *shogun* (meaning supreme general or generalissimo) and established his military government in Kamakura in 1192. With another seat of government in the same country, there was frustration inside the imperial court in Kyoto (formerly called Heian-kyo). This frustration erupted after the assassination of the third shogun, Minamoto no Sanetomo.

• *Battle of Dan-no-ura. The final stage of the Gempei War.*

• *Minamoto no Yoritomo.*

The establishment of a military government coincided with an important cultural change that had been occurring in broader society. That is, a gradual transition from admiration of the gentleman and the scholar to a new respect for loyalty and honor among warriors. *Bushido*, "the code of the warrior," encompasses the ideals of courage, duty, and self-sacrifice expected of a samurai. This way of thinking became deeply ingrained in the Japanese psychology, and to this day it is evident in various aspects of Japanese society.

The Hojo clan had plotted this assassination. Hojo was the family of Yoritomo's wife. After the success of their plot, the Hojo took the leadership of the Kamakura government as regent. Assuming that Sanetomo's assassination had caused political turmoil in Kamakura, the imperial army in 1221 took the opportunity to attack the Kamakura military government. But the shogun's forces prevailed and defeated the imperial troops.

After this battle, even though the emperor continued to be respected as the highest figure in Japanese society, the actual executive role was held by the shogun. This system lasted until 1868, when the Meiji Restoration ushered in a modern form of government.

• *Tsurugaoka Hachiman Shrine in Kamakura.*

9. Creation of People's Buddhism

During the Kamakura Period (1185–1333), many new Buddhist sects were established. Among the most important was Jodo-shu, or the Pure Land Sect. Jodo-shu originated in the tenth century as Jodo-kyo, became known as Jodo-shu under the priest Honen, and was further developed by the priest Shinran as Jodo-shinshu, or the New Pure Land Sect, in 1224.

The central tenet of Jodo-shinshu held that, if people repeat the *Nembutsu* chant, they would be saved after death because of the boundless mercy of Amida, one of the sacred figures of Buddhism. In addition, Jodo-shinshu believed that this world is like an illusion, that nobody or nothing lasts forever, so just to believe and to utter the Nembutsu meant salvation after death. Jodo-shinshu was quite popular because of its simple philosophy. And it responded to the needs of the era, when society was unstable because of war, disease, and poverty.

• *Main gate of Kencho-ji temple.*

Nichiren-shu, another sect established in the thirteenth century, by the priest Nichiren, centered on recitation of Hoke-kyo, or the Lotus Sutra, a key Buddhist text. Nichiren was an exclusivist and criticized other religious sects that did not follow his beliefs and practices. After he warned the Kamakura officials that there would be a national crisis, such as invasion by a foreign country (Mongolia, in fact, sent troops to Japan soon thereafter), he also became widely known as a prophet. His activities were so aggressive that he was prosecuted several times by the Kamakura government.

These new sects can be compared to dissenters against the Roman Catholic Church in medieval Europe, because they questioned traditional Buddhism for its great wealth, bureaucratic ways, corruption, and political influence. While traditional Buddhism and the government saw these sects as threats, vast numbers of ordinary people accepted them as more intimate and simpler to understand than the old Buddhism which had required rig-

• *Sharira hall of Engaku-ji temple.*

• *Garden of Nanzen-ji temple.*

• *Rock-garden of Ryoan-ji temple.*

orous study and training. As a result, they soon entered the mainstream of Japanese Buddhism.

Another important sect, Zen, was introduced to Japan from the Song Dynasty in China in the thirteenth century. Zen values the disciplines of meditation and physical training to overcome the troubles of daily life. Because of

Gardens in particular played an important role as settings for meditation. Nanzen-ji, Ryoan-ji, and Daitoku-ji in Kyoto are the most important Zen temples featuring such beautiful gardens. In Kamakura, there are Kencho-ji and Engaku-ji, among others.

Jodo-shu, Nichiren-shu and Zen are even now the three largest Buddhist sects in Japan.

• *Main gate of Daitoku-ji temple.*

• *Bronze of Nichiren.*

its stoic way of thought, Zen was widespread among the samurai class which emphasized strict mental and physical discipline. Many Zen temples, which are particularly numerous in Kamakura and Kyoto, were built between the twelfth and fifteenth centuries and were supported by powerful warriors. They were not only beautiful for their architecture, sculpture, and painting, but for their gardens.

10. MONGOLIAN INVASION
AND THE FALL OF KAMAKURA

During the time when new sects of Buddhism were proliferating in Japan, China experienced a massive attack from northern tribes. First, the Manchurian tribes invaded the northern part of China and then overthrew the Song Dynasty in the south. A second wave of invasions came from Mongolia, taking the territory of Manchuria and establishing a new empire, the Yuan Dynasty, in the northern half of China.

The Mongolian empire had been vast, extending to the Middle East and even into Europe. After they founded the Yuan Dynasty in north China, Kublai Khan, the strongest of the Yuan emperors, targeted Japan for takeover. On his first attempt in 1274, he sent 30,000 Korean and Mongolian troops with quite advanced weapons such as gunpowder.

However, a typhoon with heavy winds forced their ships back and destroyed their plans. They then vanquished the Southern Song Dynasty and subjugated all of China.

Kublai Khan tried to invade Japan again in 1281 with 150,000 Korean, Mongolian and Chinese soldiers, dispatched from Korea and southern China. This was the only invasion by a foreign country on Japanese soil prior to 1945, when Japan was occupied by the allied nations after the Second World War.

How did the Japanese defend their country? First, they were well prepared. After the first invasion attempt, the Japanese had erected walls around Hakata Bay in northern Kyushu, which kept the invaders immobilized for fifty-four days on the seashore. Second, the Mongols were not used to

• *Fighting between Mongolians and a Japanese warrior.*

fighting on the sea and were annoyed by the Japanese attacking from small boats. And third, yet another typhoon suddenly came and, this time, destroyed the Mongolian navy.

Having been twice saved by timely typhoons, Japanese people took them as miracles flowing from Shintoism and its doctrine of reverence for nature and nature's power. They referred to those two typhoons as *Kamikaze*, or divine wind sent by the gods. This belief contributed to the Japanese notion of their own uniqueness—that is, that the Japanese were a divinely favored tribe—and was also used as part of the militarist propaganda in the years leading to World War II.

After failing twice, the Mongols did not attack Japan again. However, this war activity brought one noteworthy result to Europe. The Italian merchant Marco Polo who served the Yuan Dynasty around this period of war, introduced Japan to the West as the land of gold and thus stimulated Europeans to travel to Asia. The Mongolian invasions also damaged the Kamakura shogunate economically and caused unrest in Japanese society. No talented leaders arose who could resolve the economic and political problems inside the government after the Mongol invasions.

Finally, some powerful supporters inside the shogunate left and joined the imperial court to oppose the Kamakura government. After several years of turbulence, the Nitta and Ashikaga clans, the most powerful in the Kamakura government, decided

• *Kublai Khan.*

to betray the Kamakura side. Thus, the Hojo clan, the actual power in the Kamakura shogunate, perished, and its government came to an end in 1333. Simultaneously, the imperial court in Kyoto established a new government under the leadership of the Emperor Godaigo.

11. Era of the Two Courts

When the Kamakura shogunate fell, the emperor's desire was to re-establish the authority of the imperial court as in ancient Japan. However, this attempt, known as *Kemmu no Chuko*, or the Kemmu Restoration, quickly failed, as it did not fit with the reality of samurai society in the fourteenth century. The Ashikaga clan, supported by the samurai, finally wiped out the new government in Kyoto and created another imperial court with one of the branches of the imperial family. Meanwhile, the Emperor Godaigo escaped to Yoshino, south of Nara, and set up the so-called "Southern Court" in 1336.

At the same time, the imperial court in Kyoto appointed Ashikaga Takauji, head of the Ashikaga clan, as the new shogun. Thus, the Ashikaga shogunate was established in Kyoto. This government was called the Muromachi

• *Emperor Godaigo.*

• *Ashikaga Yoshimitsu.*

Bakufu (*bakufu* means military government), named after the place where it was located.

This era of two courts, with two emperors, is called *Nambokucho*, or the Southern and Northern Courts, named after a similar period in Chinese history. The first thirty years brought a number of critical challenges for the Ashikaga shogunate. Perhaps the biggest trouble came from the Yamana clan, former allies of Takauji who had changed their allegiance to support the Southern Court. One Yamana leader in particular, Kitabatake Chikafusa, devoted his energies to the cause of re-establishing Godaigo as the legitimate emperor. His excellent planning and use of guerrilla tactics to surprise and confuse Takauji's forces occupied much of the Ashikaga shogunate's attention. Meanwhile, a quarrel between Takauji and his brother caused internal conflict, further weakening the cause of the

• *Ashikaga Takauji.*

mise that imperial succession would alternate between the lines of the Southern and Northern Courts. He also persuaded the imperial court to confer on him the highest rank, even among the aristocrats' hierarchy. He later reneged on his promise, ignoring the Godaigo family line (it supplied no further emperors), but his power had been consolidated and the Ashikaga clan was in control.

Northern Court.

This chaos was finally brought under control around time of the third Ashikaga shogun, Yoshimitsu. He had been appointed shogun in 1368 when he was only eleven years old. However, he gradually demonstrated a deft political talent to control the major samurai clans and to establish his iron-clad dictatorship.

Yoshimitsu persuaded the Southern Court to return to Kyoto in 1392 by agreeing to a compro-

• *Bronze of Kusunoki Masashige. He was a powerful warrior general to support the Southern Court.*

12. FROM PROSPERITY TO CHAOS

Once his governmental power was established in Kyoto, Ashikaga Yoshimitsu staunchly supported Zen temples in Kyoto and Kamakura. In Kyoto, he backed the construction of a se-

• *Kinkaku-ji temple.*

ries of large Zen temples, including Nanzen-ji, Daitoku-ji, Tenryu-ji, Myoshin-ji, Tofuku-ji and many others. He also constructed his famous villa, Kinkaku-ji, or the Temple of the Golden Pavilion, inside the Rokuon-ji temple grounds. This gold-foiled villa is one of the most popular tourist attractions in Kyoto. This era marked the height of a magnificent Buddhist culture, called Kitayama, or Northern Mountain, because Yoshimitsu's villa was located at the foot of the mountains north of Kyoto.

Toward the end of the fifteenth century, the Ashikaga shogunate was in decline, for several reasons. One was that internal power struggles escalated, giving the powerful clans a chance to assert themselves in the central government. Not only the powerful samurai clans, but also monks from temples that were supported by the Ashikaga shogunate started to exercise their own influence on the central government.

During the Ashikaga era, local major samurai clans, which were originally appointed as local governors by the Kamakura shogunate, extended their political power in their respective rural areas. The Ashikaga shogunate was considered as the power center that would unite and control those clans. Ashikaga's internal conflicts, however, gave an opportunity for the clan lords to become independent. When the Onin War broke out in 1467 and lasted until 1477, it inflicted fatal damage on the Ashikaga government. This decade-long war was waged among the major samurai clans in Kyoto, and many parts of the beautiful capital were burned and

• *Ginkaku-ji temple.*

destroyed during the fighting.

During these struggles, Ashikaga Yoshimasa, the eighth shogun, escaped to the eastern mountainside of Kyoto and created the villa called Ginkaku-ji, or the Temple of the Silver Pavilion. In his villa he focused on art and theater, because he was tired of politics and battles. It was at this time, under Yoshimasa's patronage, that the *No* theater (the traditional Japanese theater presented in a stylized form combining physical movement, music and chant) was developed by Kan'ami and his son Zeami.

In fact, many of Kyoto's temples are now located in the moun-

• *Noh stage.*

tains and hills north and east of the city, as those areas were relatively safe from the skirmishes of the Onin War. After the Onin War, the shogun was considered merely as the supreme symbol of samurai hierarchy, while local lords fought each other to expand their influence and territory. This started the era of the Hundred-Year Civil War.

• *A scene of the Onin War.*

13. THE HUNDRED-YEAR CIVIL WAR

Soon after the Ashikaga shogunate lost its political power in the late fifteenth century, major local lords created their own legal and political system to govern their respective territories. They acted as if they were independent countries, and, because of their power, Japanese rural areas were extensively developed. In the major cities governed by local lords, the markets were wide open. Kyoto's sophisticated culture and even foreign cultures were widely introduced in local areas.

It was a time of diversity and opportunity. As the medieval system declined due to the weakened central leadership, the old hierarchical system itself was gradually changing. This trend can be seen in the politics of local lords. It became relatively common for lower ranking samurai to take power from higher samurai and become new lords themselves. With greater decentralization, economic and cultural activity throughout Japan was reinvigorated.

This decentralization resulted in the proliferation of provincial and castle towns. One of these new towns, called Sakai, located just south of Osaka, grew rapidly and eventually became a sort of "free city." It had gained enough importance and power as a trading center that it was able to bargain as a corporate entity with the *bakufu* government. Sakai gained some freedom to administer its own laws, and at one time the *bakufu* even borrowed money from the merchants of the city.

Trade with China increased greatly during this time, being centered in Sakai and nearby Hyogo, current Kobe. One of the most important imports from China was copper money. Japan was not at this time minting its own coins, so the expanding trade industry relied on Chinese coins for currency. Iron, textiles, drugs, books, and art were some of the other goods imported during this

• *China-bound Japanese trading ship.*

• *Uesugi Kenshin.*

• *Takeda Shingen.*

period. The export trade from Japan was very profitable, as Japanese goods sold in the Chinese market for five to ten times their value at home. Popular exports included weapons such as swords and luxury items like lacquer-ware and fans.

During the first half of the sixteenth century, there were many battles and some powerful new lords aligned with much bigger powers, such as the lord of Shimazu in southern Kyushu, the lord of Mori in the Chugoku region, the lord of Takeda in central Honshu, the lord of Uesugi in Hokuriku, the lord of Hojo in Kanto, and the lord of Date in Tohoku.

• *Date Masamune.*

14. Introduction of Western Culture

One of the most enriching aspects of this period was global exchange. The Protestant Reformation in sixteenth-century Europe caused serious conflicts there. In addition, with the Ottoman Empire in Turkey expanding its influence into Europe, European powers felt that the economic and cultural exchange route between East and West was greatly restricted. As a result, Catholic nations such as Portugal, Spain and Italy, hoping to expand their religious influence beyond Europe, explored an ocean route to the

• *Francis Xavier.*

East. China at this time had been united after the Ming Dynasty replaced the Mongolian Yuan Dynasty around 1368. Ashikaga Yoshimitsu opened an official trade relationship with Ming China in 1404.

Trade was conducted officially and sometimes illegally. Japanese pirates, called *Wokou* (*Wako* in

Japanese), were well known in China, because they even plundered the Chinese coast. Many local lords in western and southern Japan, wealthy merchants and some large temples sent private trade missions to Korea and China. The Ming Dynasty's prosperity also attracted Europeans to China and many of them settled in southern China. This was especially true after the discovery of the ocean route to Asia. Among the most numerous and influential of the Europeans in Asia were the Portuguese, who landed on the island called Tanega-shima, located off southern Kyushu, in 1543. They introduced firearms and related technology to Japan. Like paper, powder and firearms had been invented in ancient China and introduced to Europe, where they were developed into powerful weapons.

The Portuguese also introduced Christianity to Japan, in 1549, when the Jesuit priest Francis Xavier arrived after preaching in other Asian countries. Many Japanese lords quickly accepted Christianity; some became sincere believers, while others were concerned more with trade and technological advantages. The Jesuit Valignano reported to Rome in 1582 that there were 150,000 Christians and two hundred churches in Japan. In the same year, a delegation of Japanese

• *"Southern Barbarians."*

Christian converts of noble lineage were sent to visit the Pope and the king of Spain.

The Jesuit priests were particularly successful in Kyoto, forging relationships with many influential lords. The Buddhist authorities there, alarmed at Christianity's success, brought sufficient pressure on the government to have the priests kicked out of the capital. The priests retreated to Sakai, but their message was not as successful with the merchants there.

• *Ming China's coast guards battled against Wokou.*

15. REUNIFICATION

The period of the encounter with Western culture is also the period when Japan was reunified. Around 1550, Japan was divided, the major lords having gradually expanded their territory and absorbed the jurisdictions of weaker lords.

After a series of battles, Oda Nobunaga, the lord of Owari (current area of Nagoya) sent his armies into Kyoto to take control from the Ashikaga shogunate. Nobunaga succeeded, expelling Ashikaga Yoshiaki, the fifteenth Ashikaga shogun, from Kyoto in 1573. This ended the Muromachi Bakufu and the Ashikaga line, as Nobunaga did not choose a successor for Yoshiaki. Neither did Nobunaga take the title of shogun for himself, preferring to support the imperial line while maintaining military power. Nobunaga was one of the most popular military dictators in Japanese history. He was the son of a minor lord in Owari and expanded his territory rapidly. He was a genius at military strategy and an aggressive leader. He welcomed Western influence and used it to enrich his territory. He valued the power of firearms and used them effectively when he and his ally, Tokugawa Ieyasu, defeated the Takeda clan, a powerful rival, in 1575.

Nobunaga then relocated his headquarters in Azuchi, on the shore of Lake Biwa near Kyoto, and started the process of reunification.

Azuchi had an international atmosphere, with several European missionaries residing there. Azuchi Castle was even known in Rome for its magnificent appearance. To reunify the country, he clashed with Buddhist authorities, who had not only religious but political influence.

Next he began the process of

• *Oda Nobunaga.*

subjugating the outlying regions. However, while his troops invaded the territory of the powerful Mori, the lord of western Honshu, he was betrayed by one of his own generals, Akechi Mitsuhide. While Nobunaga was passing through Kyoto on a holiday in 1582, Akechi took him by surprise in a temple called Honno-ji. To avoid capture, Nobunaga committed suicide and his body was destroyed as the temple burned to the ground.

• *Ruins of Azuchi Castle.*

• *Battle of Nagashino. In this battle Nobunaga defeated the Takeda clan.*

16. TOYOTOMI HIDEYOSHI AND HIS ERA

The general who fulfilled Nobunaga's dream was Toyotomi Hideyoshi. He had been promoted by Nobunaga from the lowest rank of samurai to become one of his top generals. At the time of Nobunaga's death, Hideyoshi was leading the battle against Mori in the western region. When he heard of Nobunaga's death, he quickly concluded a peace treaty with Mori and rushed back to Kyoto to avenge his leader's death by defeating Akechi. He then conducted several expeditions to unite Japan, and in 1590 his (and Nobunaga's) dream was realized with the fall of the Hojo clan.

Toyotomi Hideyoshi's government was different from the former military governments in that he was considered simply as the highest-ranking lord. In other words, his authority did not come from the centralized government supported by local governors (who had been appointed), each with his own jurisdiction and military system. They respected Hideyoshi as a brilliant general and as the supreme dictator. In that capacity, Hideyoshi united the system of weights and measures, surveyed land, and created his own tax system. Also, he strictly divided the people by social class and by job and prohibited the non-samurai classes from possessing weapons. Hideyoshi

• *Toyotomi Hideyoshi.*

• *Sen no Rikyu.*

placed his headquarters in Osaka where he built Osaka Castle. He also had luxurious villas in Kyoto where he controlled the temples and the imperial court.

The era of Nobunaga and Hideyoshi is called Azuchi-Momoyama, a period when certain of the traditional Japanese art forms achieved their highest expression. Many paintings were created on the walls and sliding doors of castles, temples and villas; including works by the Kano school painters—the most influential of the time. The tea ceremony was refined by Sen no Rikyu, the famous merchant and tea master who served Hideyoshi.

• *Jurakudai, Hideyoshi's residence in Kyoto.*

Painting and the tea ceremony were integrated into the lifestyles of the noble class. Many merchants and artists, on the other hand, appreciated the exotic Western culture. The city of Sakai, known as a free international trading city, was governed by merchants until Nobunaga took control. Ironically, during the civil war, the Japanese economy and lifestyle improved greatly, because of the investment of powerful local lords. When Nobunaga and Hideyoshi expanded their territory, they also received the benefits of those investments and were able to create a strong financial foundation.

By contrast, Hideyoshi's political career was not as successful. He tried twice to invade Korea, hoping to take over the Ming Dynasty in China. His first attempt was in 1592. He sent 150,000 soldiers to the Korean Peninsula. Although they captured Seoul and Pyongyang, they were forced to withdraw by a guerrilla-style counterattack supported by Chinese troops and the Korean navy. Hideyoshi's second attempt to invade Korea collapsed in transit because of his death in 1598. These invasions were known as *Bunroku-Keicho no Eki*, or the Korean Invasions in the Years of Bunroku and Keicho, by Japanese, and known as *Imjin Waeran* (*Jinshin Waran* in Japanese), or the Japanese Invasions in the Year of Imjin, by Koreans and were sometimes mentioned in connection with the annexation of Korea by Japan in 1910.

• *Koreans are attacking a Japanese fort.*

Chapter IV: Shogun and Seclusion
17. Creation of the Tokugawa Shogunate

When Hideyoshi was on his deathbed, his son Hideyori was still a small child. Hideyoshi appointed five regents to look after Hideyori until he was old enough to take the reins of leadership. The regent with the strongest influence was Tokugawa Ieyasu, lord of the Kanto area in the central part of Honshu. He was born in Mikawa, east of Nagoya, the son of a minor lord. When Oda Nobunaga, the most powerful general of the time, expanded his territory, Ieyasu supported Nobunaga's ambition.

• *Tokugawa Ieyasu.*

When Nobunaga, who had a reputation as a ruthless leader, was assassinated, Ieyasu had already become quite powerful. To acknowledge this, Hideyoshi gave Ieyasu the Kanto territory of the

• *Donjon of Osaka Castle.*

Hojo clan, which Hideyoshi had taken in 1590. This move was beneficial to Hideyoshi because it moved Ieyasu further from the capital, reducing any threat to Hideyoshi's supremacy. However, the Kanto region was already well developed as an agricultural and industrial region, and it gave Ieyasu the freedom and means to develop his own power base.

Although Ieyasu did not oppose Hideyoshi's leadership, he had become quite influential and ambitious by the time of Hideyoshi's death. Ishida Mitsunari, the top bureaucrat in Hideyoshi's government, felt the threat of Ieyasu's influence and ambition and actively opposed him.

They finally clashed in 1600 in the famous Battle of Sekigahara, between Nagoya and Kyoto, with Ieyasu defeating Mitsunari's allied

• *Ishida Mitsunari.*

Many of the events at the turn of the seventeenth century provide the background of the best-selling novel *Shogun*, written by James Clavell. This series of events, from Nobunaga's rise to the demise of Hideyori in 1615, has been fictionalized by many Japanese novelists. The story remains one of the most popular historical dramas on Japanese television.

The Tokugawa shogunate lasted until 1868, when the emperor was restored to power and Japan started to modernize under the new Meiji government.

army. After executing Mitsunari, Ieyasu established his headquarters in Edo (current Tokyo). In 1603, the emperor appointed Ieyasu as shogun. He fully consolidated his power in 1615 with his attack on Osaka Castle, which resulted in the suicide of Toyotomi Hideyori, Hideyoshi's son.

• *Battle of Sekigahara.*

18. THE FOUNDATION OF THE TOKUGAWA SHOGUNATE

The most important task for Ieyasu and his successors was to create a firm political foundation. Based on the experience of the civil war, they tried to establish a strong centralized government to control all local lords under their authority. The lords who had been Tokugawa loyalists before the Battle of Sekigahara were appointed to high office and given many privileges. Other lords were relocated to rural areas and not only removed from the seat of power but also watched carefully as they were considered potential sources of trouble.

Tokugawa built a huge castle and other buildings in Edo, the administrative center of the Tokugawa Bakufu, and appointed his closest relatives as the lords of Wakayama (south of Osaka), Owari (Nagoya) and Mito (north of Edo) to oversee and protect these important strategic areas. Unfortunately, many of the government buildings and even Edo Castle itself have been destroyed more than once by fires (even including the bombing campaign during World War II). The site of the origi-

• *Edo Castle.*

• *Niju-bashi bridge of Edo Castle.*

nal Edo Castle continues to be used as the current Imperial Palace.

The shogun also established a representative office in Kyoto to keep an eye on the activities of the imperial court, even though, in theory, the emperor was regarded as a divinity. As part of its authoritarian strategy, the Tokugawa Bakufu owned approximately 25% of available land in Japan, dividing the rest of it among the lords. These territories were called *han*.

To create social stability, Ieyasu also tightened the social struc-

• *Sakurada-mon gate of Edo Castle.*

ture along Confucianist lines to fit the feudal governmental system. He divided the nation into four classes, with samurai being the highest, then farmers, craftsmen, and merchants as the lowest. All manner of social activities, such as intermarriage between classes, the changing of jobs, movement from one class to another or even relocating were either prohibited or strictly controlled. This was accomplished by means of a detailed registration system and enforced by the police. The shogun also imposed the rule of group accountability—in other words, if someone committed a crime, not only that individual but also his or her family and sometimes neighbors were prosecuted.

• *Sakurada-bori moat of Edo Castle.*

19. Closing the Nation

The Tokugawa strategy had a huge impact on Japanese history. Confucianism was brought to Japan from China during the late Yamato Period, and the Tokugawa rulers eventually adopted it in its Neo-Confucian form to support the feudal social system. It was accepted rapidly by samurai society to undergird basic morality and models of behavior. In fact, Neo-Confucianism became the essential educational tool used to establish and maintain social stability.

In particular, the sense of class, of hierarchy, of centralized government and bureaucracy, and of group-oriented behavior still remain as important structural and social values in Japan that distinguish it from more individualistic Western societies. For example, even now, whether in public office or in private business, if a subordinate makes a serious mistake or commits a crime, his or her boss is considered to be responsible, too.

The deepest influence on the modern Japanese mentality was Japan's isolation from the rest of the world. The Tokugawa shogunate closed Japan's door to foreign countries in 1639, except for Dutch, Chinese and Korean envoys. Even they were restricted to the small artificial island called Dejima in Nagasaki. This policy was inspired by the concern of Ieyasu and his successors over the territorial ambitions of Western nations. In addition, with Christianity's rapid growth, they feared that it was like an advance army with the goal of converting Japan to a colony.

By the beginning of the seventeenth century, the Dutch and British started to expand their trading influence into Asia. The Spanish and Portuguese had already opened their headquarters in Manila and Macao, respectively, to stimulate their trade and religious relationships with Asians. Both countries had a big presence in Japan. The Dutch and British, however, took a different approach than their Catholic rivals, because they were interested only in trade, not in missionary work. They persuaded the Tokugawa government to push their Catholic rivals out of Japan. Nevertheless, the British could not make money

• *Dejima.*

42

enough in Japan and they closed their trading post, located in Hirado in western Kyushu, in 1623.

The Tokugawa government was quite serious in its prohibition of Christianity. Countless Japanese Christians faced martyrdom, unless they recanted their belief. The persecutions of Christians came to a dramatic climax in 1637, when Christian followers and farmers, who suffered under a heavy tax burden, rebelled in Shimabara, near Nagasaki. This rebellion lasted about one year, and over a hundred thousand soldiers were dispatched by the Tokugawa government to quell the uprising.

After this rebellion, the government tightened its persecution and took stronger action against its Catholic trading partners. The Portuguese were ejected in 1639, and all Japanese living abroad were prohibited from returning home. In fact, during the first two decades of the seventeenth century, many Japanese sailed to Southeast Asia where they created Japanese settlements and conducted trade with local merchants as well as Europeans. Also, some lords, like Date, of Sendai, sent envoys to Western countries. Such activities were strictly prohibited when the seclusion policy was promulgated in 1639. This policy continued until 1854, when the Tokugawa shogu-

• *Dutch ship.*

nate opened Japan's door under the pressure of Commodore Matthew Perry's visit to Japan in his Black Ships.

The benefit of this seclusion was the stability of the Tokugawa political and social institutions for more than two hundred years. Its drawback, however, was far-reaching: Japan was so far behind Western countries that it was almost impossible to catch up. Japan paid the price for this in the last part of the nineteenth and in the twentieth centuries. Even more profound, this long seclusion gave the Japanese a complex sense of their own uniqueness, that they were a homogeneous island tribe different from all other peoples. This conviction persists in Japan today and is often cited as a reason for the Japanese inability to communicate globally.

20. THE PERIOD OF KABUKI AND UKIYO-E

Under the seclusion policy and the stable Tokugawa rule, Japanese enjoyed domestic prosperity. Cities prospered and the merchant class developed a money-based economy. Around the beginning of the eighteenth century, more than one million people lived in Edo, making it the world's largest city.

Supported by wealthy merchants and a vigorous economy, Edo cultural activity flourished. Kabuki (theater presented in a grand, stylized, actor-centered spectacle) emerged and became a sophisticated performing art around the end of the seventeenth

• *A Kabuki actor in ukiyo-e by Toshusai Sharaku.*

• *Kabuki.*

century. To celebrate Kabuki actors, printed wooden brochures were widely circulated and became recognized as an art form called *ukiyo-e* (the wood-block

print pictures of the "floating world"). In the late nineteenth century, the style of these prints had a profound impact on Western impressionist painters.

With the invention of a method of color wooden printing in 1765 by Suzuki Harunobu, ukiyo-e took on a more sophisticated form as a graphic commercial art. Kitagawa Utamaro, Katsushika Hokusai and Toshusai Sharaku were among the most popular artists in the eighteenth and early nineteenth centuries. Publishing was also quite active. Love stories and tragic tales with samurai heroes were widely circulated and adapted for Kabuki and the Bunraku puppet theater.

Edo period cultural activity

had two peaks. The first began toward the end of the seventeenth century during the years of the fifth Tokugawa shogun, Tsunayoshi, and was called the Genroku era. It was a time of relative prosperity. In fact, because of the "Pax Tokugawa," the martial skills of

• *Ukiyo-e.*

the samurai became less and less necessary. Many samurai took jobs as civilian bureaucrats and came to prefer a relatively more extravagant lifestyle to that of the traditional warrior. This trend coincided with the burgeoning middle class city life of Edo. The Genroku era also saw the emergence of *haiku*, the seventeen-syllable poem. Matsuo Basho is well-known as the one who developed this poetic form.

The second cultural peak in the Edo Period was in the late eighteenth century, the Bunka Bunsei era. Cultural activity was vital not only in Edo but also in Kansai (the area including Osaka and Kyoto.) For example, Chikamatsu Monzaemon, a famous playwright, adapted many famous stories for Bunraku and Kabuki in the Kansai area. It was also around this time that Western ships started to wander near the coast to knock on the door of an isolated Japan. This eventually stimulated some scholars to travel to Nagasaki to study Western culture through the Dutch language.

• *Matsuo Basho.*

21. Decline of the Feudal System

Around the latter part of the eighteenth century, the social system created by Tokugawa started to show signs of decline, particularly through certain changes in the economy. Big cities were already operating under a money-based economy, while domain lords were receiving tax on the rice crop grown by their vassals. Salaries for their samurai were paid in rice, based on the feudal system. So they needed to exchange rice for money to survive. In fact, it was becoming quite common for city merchants to finance lords and samurai, who were gradually building up debt to the merchants (considered the lowest social class in the Tokugawa feudal system).

The situation was even more severe for rural lords. The shogunate kept them under tight control by imposing many financial obligations. One of these, *sankin kotai*, required all lords, ostensibly for security reasons, to stay in Edo every other year. It was very costly for them to travel to Edo and back to their home province each year. Adding to their burden was the cost of maintaining both their Edo domicile and their outlying territories.

Many lords tried to improve their financial situation. For example, Satsuma *han*, now Kagoshima prefecture, secretly conducted foreign trade through Okinawa.

However, many lords simply failed. They were also concerned about rebellious farmers who protested against heavy taxes. In fact, many samurai became jobless and sometimes even homeless as a result of Tokugawa's strategy. The class of peasant farmers were abused and neglected throughout the Tokugawa Period. The government had a policy of allowing farmers to keep just enough of their harvests to stay alive until the next year—the rest of the produce was taken as tax. Additionally, famines plagued the peasants throughout this era. The three major famines of 1732, 1783, and 1832 in particular brought intense suffering. As a result, it is no wonder that peasant uprisings and rebellions were fre-

• *Procession of a daimyo.*

• *British troops in the Battle of Shimonoseki.*

quent.

From the very beginning of the Tokugawa era, the shogunate, sensing potential problems with those lords who gave allegiance to the Tokugawa only after the Battle of Sekigahara, made things difficult for them. As a result, many of those lords lost their territory and the thousands of samurai who served them also lost their livelihood. Such jobless samurai were called *ronin*, and they were ubiquitous. For samurai, the highest social rank, to be in dire financial straits, created a basic contradiction in Tokugawa society. The growing, powerful merchant class, large numbers of unemployed samurai, and continuous peasant rebellions created major internal problems for the Tokugawa rulers. This contradiction was compounded by another challenge: the appearance of foreign battleships.

• *Emperor Komei.*

• *Ii Naosuke, Tokugawa's Prime Minister.*

22. Opening of the Nation and the Fall of Tokugawa

In the eighteenth century, some foreign ships had appeared in Japan and tried to re-ignite trade relationships. But the Tokugawa government had stubbornly kept its policy of seclusion. However, when the four U.S. frigates commanded by Commodore Matthew

• *Commodore Matthew Perry.*

Perry arrived in Uraga Bay near Edo in 1853, the Tokugawa government suddenly realized that Japan had been sleeping unaware of what was happening around it.

Four battleships with their advanced weapons were quite enough to put pressure on the government to modify its policies. After long negotiations, the Tokugawa leaders finally decided to open their door again in 1854. They opened several ports and started trade relationships, first with the U.S., then with Russia,

France, England and the Netherlands.

The weak reaction of the Tokugawa government was severely criticized by many Japanese nationalists, who blamed the government because this important decision was made without reporting it to the imperial court. The nationalists thought the emperor must be respected as Japan's supreme ruler, even though actual administrative power belonged to the Tokugawa shogunate. Many samurai and even some lords held nationalist ideas and strongly urged the shogunate to fight against the so-called "barbarian pressure."

Since the Tokugawa leaders knew that Western imperialism was colonizing Asian lands by using advanced military power and technology, they tried to suppress the people who were opposed to their decision. Thus, the nation was divided into two groups: those who opposed Tokugawa's foreign policy and those who supported the old feudal government.

• *Perry's "Black Ships."*

• *Tokugawa Yoshinobu.*

Kyoto, where the imperial court was located, became the center of this turmoil.

As for political power, Satsuma (now Kagoshima prefecture, located in southern Kyushu) and Choshu (now Yamaguchi prefecture, located in western Honshu) had become the most influential *han*, as their lords successfully promoted talented samurai to influential positions in the central government. These were the new leaders who put Japan on its new, modern course. Initially, they tried to remove foreign influence from Japan and even fought against the Western powers. However, when the Western navies successfully attacked these two *han*, the Japanese learned the necessity of developing advanced military power and technology.

In implementing this strategy, Satsuma and Choshu led the ef-fort to overthrow the old Tokugawa power. After a series of battles, assassinations and other turmoil, these two *han* joined in 1866 to create an allied front against Tokugawa and were secretly supported by the imperial court. The coordinator of this alliance was Sakamoto Ryoma of Tosa (now Kochi prefecture in southern Shikoku), who was unfortunately assassinated after this secret agreement was made. The shogun was too weak economically and militarily to withstand the new movement.

Under this heavy pressure, Tokugawa Yoshinobu, the last shogun, resigned in 1867. At that point, the anti-Tokugawa forces tried to establish a new government under the authority of the imperial court. But Yoshinobu did not give up without a fight. After he resigned, he concentrated his forces at Osaka Castle to oppose the anti-Tokugawa alliance led by Saigo Takamori, one of the distinguished new leaders of Satsuma. By 1868, Saigo defeated the Tokugawa forces in the Kyoto suburbs of Toba and Fushimi. After escaping to Edo, Yoshinobu surrendered, and the feudal era of rule by shogun finally came to an end.

Chapter V: The Meiji Period

23. MEIJI RESTORATION

The year 1868 was one of the most important in modern Japanese history. It was the year Japan officially started to become a modern state. The new imperial government swept away all opposition forces still loyal to the old Tokugawa government. Even as Tokugawa Yoshinobu surrendered, some lords persistently tried to fight back against the new imperial government. This series of battles between the new government and the Tokugawa supporters was called the Boshin Civil War. The most famous battle was in Aizu-Wakamatsu in Tohoku, where many samurai were killed and wounded. By April 1869, the last of the Tokugawa supporters was defeated in Hakodate, Hokkaido.

The new government decided to move the imperial court from Kyoto to Edo, which was renamed Tokyo as the new capital of a reformed Japan. The task of the new government was obvious: to create Japan as an advanced nation with a strong military and vigorous industry. When the Emperor Komei died in 1866, the Emperor Meiji officially succeeded to the throne in September 1867. This is known as *Meiji-Ishin* or the Meiji Restoration.

A stable government was needed for both domestic and international reasons. To avoid the fate of many other Asian nations, which were colonized by the Western powers, Japan's new leaders tried to plant modern technology, military power and administrative systems in Japanese soil. Under the leadership of Kido Takayoshi, Okubo Toshimichi, Iwakura Tomomi, Saigo Takamori and some other new leaders, social class distinctions and samurai privilege were abolished.

The government began to recruit soldiers from among ordinary

• *Battle of Aizu-Wakamatsu in the Boshin Civil War.*

• *Emperor Meiji.*

Restoration, Japan had been iso-lated for more than 230 years—a period during which the Japanese had developed a distinctive set of values and ethics.

Now Japan was opened. And the new leadership started reform by absorbing foreign technology. Of course, technology cannot be imported without having the val-ues and ethics of other peoples attached to it. The mixture of a new wave from other cultures with its own traditional identity gave Japan an opportunity to move for-ward. The Meiji Period was the starting point for the Japanese en-

• *Okubo Toshimichi.*

Japanese citizens. To create cen-tralized authority, they abolished the feudal *han* system and intro-duced a system of prefectures with governors appointed by Tokyo. The old financial system was converted to a modern bank-ing and monetary system. New tax and legal policies were inte-grated under the central govern-ment. And railroad, telecommuni-cation and postal systems were established. The first rail service opened in 1872 between Tokyo and Yokohama.

All these were important steps toward realizing the government's mission to catch up with Western powers to protect the nation and its interests. Encountering a differ-ent culture can stimulate people to gain a better sense of their own identity. That is what happened in Japan. Just before the Meiji

try into World War II, because the crucible of fate and opportunity led to the emergence of national-ism. Also, the Meiji Period was an-other opportunity for the Japan-ese—a starting point to create an industrially advanced nation.

24. FROM THE SEINAN WAR
TO THE PROMULGATION OF THE MEIJI CONSTITUTION

To forge a modern nation, the Meiji government needed to overcome several challenges. The most important was to tame the frustration of former samurai who had lost their privileges. Many of them tried to foment rebellion

• *Bronze of Saigo Takamori.*

against the government. The Seinan War in 1877 was their most serious effort. It was sparked when Saigo Takamori, one of the heroes of the Meiji Restoration, left the government because of stark political differences. Many frustrated samurai and his own followers pressed Saigo to rebel. His private army eventually numbered more than thirty thousand. Their rebellion started in Kagoshima (formerly Satsuma, Saigo's homeland) and spread throughout the southern part of Kyushu. However, within several months Saigo was overwhelmed by the modernized, powerful military dispatched from Tokyo, and he committed suicide in Kagoshima.

After the Seinan War, frustrated samurai continued their protests against the government with their voices instead of weapons. They asked the government to listen to their demands. They blamed it for not introducing a representative democracy such as in Western nations. They insisted on the right to send their repre-

• *Battle of Tabaruzaka in the Seinan War.*

• Proclamation ceremony for Constitution of the Empire of Japan.

sentatives to the central government.

The Meiji government, however, felt that the people's protests might develop into further turmoil and were therefore dangerous. The government leaders wanted to create modern administrative, judicial and legislative powers under the authority of the emperor. After extensive internal confusion and argument, they finally installed a parliamentary system in 1889 with a constitution modeled after Germany's. The first imperial parliament, called the Diet, was opened the next year. The cabinet had already been created in 1885, with Ito Hirobumi appointed as the first prime minister.

In several respects, this parliamentary system was not completely democratic. For example, suffrage was given only to taxpaying males. And the upper house of the Diet was made up exclusively of aristocrats, the emperor's relatives and persons appointed by the emperor. According to the constitution, the Diet was responsible only to the emperor, who was considered the supreme authority. As with the constitution, government officials followed a European model—France—for their criminal and civil law.

Around the same time, the economy began to heat up, and manufacturing increased rapidly. Particularly vigorous were the textile and shipping industries. However, those successes were achieved because of strong governmental support for those who had special fortune and privilege. Almost all ordinary citizens and farmers remained poor. As a result, during the tortuous attempts to create a parliamentary system, the socialist movement became active. The government tried to deal with such opposition movements first by using its power to oppress them, and later by shifting its attention to foreign issues such as war and invasion.

25. WAY TO THE RUSSO-JAPANESE WAR

The nineteenth century was the era of imperialism. England, France, Germany, Russia, the Netherlands and later the U.S. were the major players to snatch territory and create spheres of influence in Asian and African nations. These Western nations had concluded unequal treaties with Japan. From the very beginning of the Meiji Period, the government's main task was to change such unfair conditions. Balance was not completely restored until after Japan was recognized as the one of the world's strongest military powers.

The Japanese saw Russia as their biggest threat because of its geographical location. Accordingly, they turned their attention first to the Korean Peninsula, because, even though Korea was considered as subordinate to the Qing Dynasty in China, the Japanese believed that strong influence in Korea would be the best way to protect Japanese interests from Russia. Thus, Japan requested Korea to open their nation, and then imposed their own unequal treaty. Finally, after manipulating Korea's internal politics, Japan forced Korea to accept a Japanese military presence. Of course, these activities provoked a war with China over control of the Korean Peninsula. The war lasted eight months, and the Westernized Japanese military easily dominated.

The Treaty of Shimonoseki, in which China agreed to give Japan Taiwan, some islands, the Liaodong Peninsula and monetary compensation for war damages, was signed between the two nations in 1895. However, Western nations, with their respective spheres of influence and assets in China, saw the Japanese victory as a new threat. Eventually, Russia, Germany and France demanded the return of the Liaodong Peninsula to the Qing Dynasty. Japan gave in to this demand, because it was too dangerous for Meiji Japan to have a hostile relationship with these powerful nations.

Still, the Japanese government used this international pressure to stimulate Japanese public opinion toward nationalism. They invested in the military and stimulated industrialization, and they continued their attempts to exercise influence in Korea.

The international power struggle in East Asia in the late nineteenth century involved nearly all the major Western countries seeking greater economic opportunity in China. When the British grasped Japan's concern about Russia's pressure, they opted to support Japan in order to defuse the Russian territorial ambition. Japan and England became allied in 1902, making official their common interest against Russia. The U.S. also supported Japan, because, following their annexation of the Philippines after the Spanish-American War in 1898, they wanted to establish an economic presence in Manchuria. France and Germany, on the other hand, were British rivals and supported Russia.

Given these difficult and complex relationships, Japan and Russia faced severe obstacles to establishing their interests in Manchuria and the Korean Peninsula. Japan finally declared war against Russia in February 1904, after ten years of preparation. This war posed great risk for Meiji Japan, as Russia was one of the reigning superpowers with vast territory, technology and military power. Although Japan clashed with the Russian army and navy in a number of severe battles and exhausted its economic resources, its efforts were heavily financed by England and the U.S.

At the same time, the Russian government feared that if they continued the war and exhausted their soldiers and economy, the growing revolutionary movement would gain momentum.

The American president, Theodore Roosevelt, offered to mediate a peace treaty. The delegations of Japan and Russia met in the U.S., at Portsmouth, New Hampshire, to negotiate. Japan took southern Sakhalin and ownership of the South Manchuria Railway. Thus, the Russo-Japanese War came to an end in 1905, after costing huge sums of money and many lives on both sides.

• *Japanese navy's Grand Fleet in the Yellow Sea.*

26. Annexation of Korea

Japan and Russia fought their war mainly in China. It was the fate of Asia that Western powers and the new player, Imperial Japan, used Asia as their chessboard. There were people who opposed war both in Japan and Russia. In Japan, Socialists and Christian activists played an important anti-war role. The Christian philosopher Uchimura Kanzo and the Socialist activist Kotoku Shusui were the most well known figures to protest against such imperialism.

However, the vast majority of Japanese were excited about Japan's triumph but also disappointed that Japan did not gain as

• *Ito Hirobumi, the Chairman of Privy Council and the Supervisor of Korea.*

much from the war as expected. The negotiation in Portsmouth was quite tough for the Japanese side, as the Russians knew Japan

had exhausted its resources and could hardly have continued the war. To counter the Japanese disappointment, to elicit respect for Japan among the Western powers, and to recover economic stability and national security, Japanese leaders like Ito Hirobumi thought that the annexation of Korea was indispensable.

When the war against Russia ended, Korea was completely under Japanese control. Korea protested to the international community, but none of the Western powers responded, because they had undertaken similar imperialist activities in India, China, the Philippines and many other Asian and African nations. Therefore, when the Japanese finally colonized Korea in 1910, there was no interference or protest by Western countries. The U.S. secretly approved Japan's actions, because Japan had approved the U.S. control of the Philippines. When Ito Hirobumi appointed Terauchi Masatake as the first governor of Korea, the Korean kingdom officially ceased to exist.

The Japanese annexation of Korea, which lasted until Japan's defeat in World War II, left deep wounds in Korea. Japanese officials responded to Korean independence movements with severe prosecution, even torture. The most famous incident, the March First Movement, occurred in 1919.

This was a massive, nationwide anti-Japanese demonstration in which over two million Koreans participated. Koreans in Japan were often the targets of discrimination. During World War II, over a hundred thousand Koreans were forced to move to Japan as laborers (and sometimes as prostitutes for the military fighting abroad). Many such Korean immigrants have continued living in Japan even after Korea's independence, and they continue to face prejudice to this day.

• *Kotoku Shusui (left) and Kanno Suga.*

• *Sunjong, the last emperor of the Empire of Korea.*

• *Terauchi Masatake, the first Governor-General of Korea.*

The Meiji Period began the modern Japanese era. Not only were Japan's political system, economy and military modernized, but an array of new cultural movements also emerged. Japan worked hard to catch up with the standards of the more technologically and socially advanced Western nations. Meiji Japan invested time and energy in the development of new educational, military, governmental and administrative systems. By the end of the Meiji Period in 1912, Western influence could be seen all over Japan, particularly in major cities, in everything from architecture to daily life.

This influence was also evident in literature and the arts. For example, the writers Natsume Soseki, who studied in London, and Mori Ogai, who studied in Germany, and many others penned many essays, stories and novels that incorporated Western literary techniques. Journalism also developed, following Western models. In fact, the Japanese word for newspaper—*shimbun*—

• *"Gakumon no Susume," or the Recommendation for Learning, one of Fukuzawa's best-selling books.*

was created in the Meiji Period by Fukuzawa Yukichi, foremost among Japan's modernizers. This was a period in which even the average Japanese person had great curiosity about the customs of the West, and Fukuzawa's

• *Mori Ogai.*

• *Building of Choya Shimbun.*

• Fukuzawa Yukichi in a bank note.

best-selling books were the authority on that subject. Throughout his life, Fukuzawa contributed greatly to the cause of education through his writings and translations, and eventually by founding Keio University, the first private university in Japan.

Christianity was officially approved in 1873, and many Japanese Christians who had studied in the U.S. and Europe played important opinion-making roles in Japan. Some of them, like Abe Isoo and Katayama Sen, applied their Christian beliefs to socialist causes after seeing the agony of poor farmers and workers. Social contradictions were in direct proportion to the accomplishments of the industrial revolution. The rich minority had the power and dominated the poor majority. Socialists and communists actively protested this situation and incurred serious oppression from the government.

With so much Western influence coming into Japan, it was perhaps inevitable that a reaction against it would set in. In an effort to protect their identity, many Japanese reacted to Western penetration with resentment and expressions of nationalism. Such expressions were often associated with state Shintoism, supported by the Meiji government with its plan to unite Japan under the emperor's glory. Nationalist inclinations linking Shintoism with the emperor's divinity eventually led Japan into World War II.

• Natsume Soseki in a bank note.

Chapter VI: Path to World War II
28. Era of Taisho Democracy

The Meiji era ended with the Emperor Meiji's death in 1912. Because of his many successes, Japan's international status had improved, and Japan had become a major player in world affairs. When the Emperor Taisho succeeded to the throne, the Japanese were actually able to enjoy their achievements. The economic damage of World War I was serious, however, and the government's solution was to raise taxes. That decision moved the public to protest and stimulated various social movements, including feminism and communism, to become active on a wide scale. In fact, the Taisho era was distinctive for its democratic atmosphere. Politically, the movement of parliamentary democracy spread throughout Japan and suffrage was finally granted to all males above the age of twenty-five in 1925. Demonstrations and political gatherings

• *Emperor Taisho.*

were legal and frequently held, but some became illegal when communism and socialism were banned in 1925.

The generally democratic Taisho atmosphere contributed to a fertile culture. Writers, such as Akutagawa Ryunosuke, Shiga Naoya, Tanizaki Junichiro and many other novelists created many of the most notable works of modern Japanese literature. Taisho also saw the dawn of the media business. Radio broadcasts started in 1925, and countless magazines and publications were launched.

In its international policies, however, Taisho was also the era when Japanese military activity started becoming aggressive. During World War I, Japan had joined the Allied forces with Eng-

• *Tanizaki Junichiro.*

• *Akutagawa Ryunosuke.*

• *Shiga Naoya.*

land, France and the U.S. While this war was fought mainly in Europe, Japan took the opportunity to expand its presence in China. The Japanese army occupied the German-controlled Shandong Peninsula and demanded that the Chinese government give Japan political and military privileges. In China, the weakened Qing Dynasty had given way to the Republic of China, and nationalism was heightened to combat foreign imperialism against their nation. The Japanese presence in China, therefore, stimulated anti-Japanese sentiments.

In fact, it was around the end of Meiji and the beginning of Taisho when Japan started to invest heavily in its military with the goal of targeting China. After Japan defeated Russia in the Russo-Japanese War of 1904–05, Japan started to expand its influence westward, particularly to China. So Japan's potential ene-

my was becoming the U.S. In 1922, at the urging of the U.S., Japan, the U.S., England, France and Italy signed the Washington Treaty to achieve armament reduction. These nations also confirmed their own rights to expand their interests toward the Pacific and China.

• *Admiral Kato Tomosaburo, the plenipotentiary to the Washington Treaty.*

29. Invasion of Manchuria

When a nation's economy is in good shape, peace can prevail. Once people start feeling the fear of poverty, however, the air often becomes polluted with threats of conspiracy and even war. When the Japanese economy after World War II had fully recovered and even expanded, the Japanese public was more interested in domestic and democratic issues. When World War I ended, however, world economic demand shrank and Japan faced serious recession.

The effort of Japanese industry to ride out the recession was nullified by two major catastrophes. In 1923, Tokyo was hit by a major earthquake that killed more than 130,000 people. This disaster smashed the possibility of economic recovery and put a heavy financial burden on the Japanese government. Six years later, the famous Wall Street crash of 1929 occurred. The Emperor Taisho had already passed away in 1926 and Japan was in the fourth year of the Emperor Showa (known outside Japan as Hirohito). The U.S. had become the world's biggest creditor nation after World War I, so the financial panic there was felt all over the world, including Japan. The damage was widespread—not only banks and heavy industries but also agriculture and retailing were severely set back. In rural areas, poor farmers even sold their daughters. And their sons tried to be recruited by the military.

To survive this chaos, Japan's major financial and industrial conglomerates, known as *zaibatsu*, strengthened their ties to government and decided to seek new markets and opportunities in China, particularly Manchuria. Zaibatsu such as Mitsui, Mitsubishi, Sumitomo, Yasuda and Daiichi had great influence on major political parties and gradually integrated with the military movement.

In 1931, the Japanese army became aggressive in Manchuria and eventually created a puppet government by appointing the dethroned emperor Pu Yi of the Qing

• *Japanese army in Mukden.*

• *Pu Yi, the emperor of Manchukuo.*

Dynasty as emperor of Manchukuo. This resulted in Japan being condemned by the international community. Since all the major countries in the League of Nations were opposed to the Japanese territorial expansion, the Japanese government decided to leave this international organization.

World War I carried many lessons for the world's major powers. They paid a tremendous price to learn how imperialism can damage people and nations. Japan also did not recognize the value of peace and co-existence in the world community and the Japanese public felt the weight of international pressure (just as Russia had prior to the Russo-Japanese War). The negative attitude of the Japanese toward the U.S. and other Western nations who had forced open Japan in the nineteenth century remained, and a fanatic nationalism developed. The military, particularly the army,

with its stubborn superiority complex, manipulated public opinion. The right wing supported such activity, while at the same time suppressing various social movements as anti-government.

In 1932, radical army soldiers assassinated Inukai Tsuyoshi, the prime minister, who headed Seiyu-kai, the majority party in the Diet. And on February 26, 1936, a group of young military officers, who were opposed to the close relationship between the zaibatsu and the government, launched a coup d'état and killed some Diet members, including Prime Minister Saito Makoto, a former naval officer. Through such disturbances, the military gradually took hegemony in the central government, and the invasion of China became more aggressive. Thus, the democratic movement created in the Taisho era was completely swept away.

• *Qinmin-lou, Pu Yi's office.*

30. WAR AGAINST CHINA

After the Japanese army took control of Manchukuo, strong anti-Japanese sentiment was widely expressed in China. This sentiment was so strong that a truce was called on the internal battle between the communists, under Mao Zedong, and the nationalists, which officially governed China under the leadership of Chiang Kai-shek. The two sides agreed in 1936 to create a united front to resist the Japanese invasion.

To crush this alliance Japan started a massive attack in 1937, beating a Chinese garrison at Lugouqiao Bridge near Beijing. The Japanese occupied Shanghai, Nanjing (the Chinese capital) and many other major cities. It was during this time that the Japanese army committed a cruel massacre in Nanjing, killing several hundred thousand Chinese soldiers and citizens. The Chinese government escaped from Nanjing to Chongqing in Sichuan, and the Japanese created a puppet government by appointing Wang Zhaoming (alias Wang Jingwei) as prime minister.

• *Lugouqiao Bridge.*

However, long drawn-out battles in the vast Chinese territory stretched the Japanese army thin. They could occupy cities but it was impossible to keep mountains and rural areas under their control. Also, the Japanese activities created serious tensions with the

• *Wang Zhaoming.*

U.S. and England, who had considerable interests in China. They officially supported China and established economic sanctions against Japan. In Manchuria, the Japanese army attacked the Soviet Union in Nomonhan in 1939 because of a territorial dispute, but Stalin's army defeated the Japanese and put strong pressure on the Japanese government not to

• *Japanese army in Shanghai.*

invade their territory again.

By now Japan was isolated from the international community and seen as inimical to the international democracy and peace movements. Japan was also seen as attempting to encroach on the Western assets created in Asia over more than three centuries.

Germany and Italy were making similarly aggressive efforts in Europe. When World War II broke out in Europe in 1939, Germany's strength was formidable. Finally, Germany, Italy and Japan became official allies with a treaty signed in 1940 under the cabinet led by Prime Minister Konoe Fumimaro. Thus, the Axis powers were established.

In response to the economic sanctions and the necessity of continuing the war against China, Japan started to invade Southeast Asia to maintain stable supply routes for oil and other resources. Japanese forces invaded French-controlled Vietnam in 1940 and 1941. This invasion resulted in the U.S. decision to ban oil exports to Japan. England and the Netherlands quickly followed the U.S. lead.

Internally, Japanese leaders manipulated public opinion and trumpeted that all Japanese must be united to overcome this national crisis. First, they passed a law called *Kokka Sodoin Ho*, or the State General Mobilization Law, in

• *Chiang Kai-shek and his wife Song Meiling.*

1938, enabling government control of all media, industry and individual citizens in order to continue the war effort. Second, in 1940 all political parties were united into one party, called *Taisei Yokusan Kai*, or the Imperial Rule Assistance Association. As a result of this new system, parliament became just a gathering to approve governmental and military decisions. To support this action, both regular police and military police closely watched anti-government movements and controlled people's daily lives. Japan became a country run as a war machine.

• *Japanese army in Tianjin.*

31. The Pacific War and World War II

The extent of Emperor Hirohito's involvement in making the final decision to invade China and wage war against the allied nations remains a mystery. Japan clearly was a nation under strong military leadership, which manipulated not only the Japanese public, but the government and the emperor himself as well. Actually, Prime Minister Konoe Fumimaro wanted to tame the military and find some compromise with the nations who had placed severe economic sanctions on Japan. Some officials, like former Prime Minister Yonai Mitsumasa and Admiral Yamamoto Isoroku, were also strongly opposed to fighting against the Western allied forces.

First, in April of 1941, to secure the northern front in Manchuria, Japan signed a neutrality treaty with the Soviet Union, which was in a tense situation with Germany. Second, Japan sent diplomatic delegations to the U.S. to attempt to ease the tensions and the economic sanctions. President Roosevelt and his secretary of state, Cordell Hull, demanded full withdrawal of the Japanese army from China. However, even during the negotiation period, the Japanese army stubbornly ignored directions from the civilian government and expanded its war effort to areas throughout

• Pearl Harbor under the air raid by Japanese naval air force.

• *Admiral Yamamoto Isoroku.*

China and Southeast Asia. This only increased tensions with the U.S. and England.

Finally, the army leader Tojo Hideki became prime minister in October 1941. He decided on a full assault against the U.S. and England and had the Japanese navy and air force attack Pearl Harbor on December 7, 1941 (it was already December 8 in Japan). The U.S. navy in Hawaii was taken by complete surprise—seven battleships and about half of the aircraft there were destroyed. Simultaneously, Japanese forces attacked Malaysia and Singapore and occupied most of Southeast Asia, including the Philippines, where a U.S. base was located. The Japanese also occupied a number of South Pacific islands. Within six months of the Pearl Harbor attack, the Japanese army was already making preparations to invade Australia.

Japanese propaganda to justify and promote their aggression was centered on the catch phrase *Dai Toa Kyoei Ken*, or the Greater East Asia Co-prosperity Sphere. It was intended to mean that Japan could help other Asian nations stand up to and be independent from Western imperialism, but it was perceived quite differently outside Japan. Ironically, if Japan had not annexed Korea and invaded China, this propaganda may have received some sympathy—but the reality was far removed from the ideology.

• *Prime Minister Tojo Hideki (right) and Prime Minister of Manchukuo Zhang Jinghui.*

32. THE ATOMIC BOMB AND SURRENDER

Japan's offensive was successful for the first six months or so. Then the U.S. navy defeated the Japanese navy in the Battle of Midway. This became the turning point in the war. American economic and military power was more substantial than Japan's. The longer the war continued, therefore, the more obvious Japan's disadvantage became.

From the South Pacific, the U.S. started a counter-offensive, gradually pushing the Japanese back to the north. In China, the Japanese army was exhausting its resources while trying to fight off endless guerrilla attacks. In Southeast Asia, England pushed the Japanese back from Burma. After taking Saipan in 1944, the U.S. air force started its bombing campaign on Japan itself and, in the Pacific, gradually overcame the Japanese navy. In response, the Japanese air force began the suicide attacks called *Kamikaze* (see Chapter Three.) By April 1945, U.S. forces started landing on Okinawa.

In Europe, Italy had already surrendered in 1943, and the allied nations were attacking Germany from both sides. In the same year, Roosevelt, Churchill and Chiang Kai-shek met in Cairo to discuss the postwar arrangements. Stalin and Roosevelt met in Yalta in February 1945 to confirm that the Soviet Union would invade Manchuria from the north, when the neutrality treaty with Japan had expired. After the fall of Nazi Germany, the allied leaders issued the Potsdam Declaration in July 1945, asking Japan to accept unconditional surrender.

The Potsdam Declaration included the elimination of militarism, the occupation of mainland Japan and the return of all foreign territories to the appropriate claimants. While Prime Minister Suzuki Kantaro delayed his response, two atomic bombs were dropped—one on Hiroshima on August 6th and one on Nagasaki on August 9th—killing more than 320,000 innocent citizens. The Soviet Union promptly declared war on Japan and invaded Manchuria.

On August 14th, after long argument and discussion, Japan's leaders decided to accept the Potsdam Declaration, and the Emperor Hirohito made the announcement to his nation on the radio. On September 2nd, the surrender was officially signed on the U.S. battleship Missouri in Tokyo Bay and the Japanese military was dismantled.

As a result, Korea became independent, Taiwan was returned to China, and southern Sakhalin was returned to the Soviet Union. Japan had suffered the loss 3.1 million lives and immeasurable damage to its land and people.

Even long after the war, atomic bomb victims in Hiroshima suffered leukemia. In China, countless Japanese children were separated from their parents when they escaped from Manchuria to Japan; many were never reunited.

Japan, as the aggressor nation, completely forfeited the trust of its Asian neighbors. Even now, many Asian countries are quite nervous about the development of the Japanese military. The essential challenge for Japan is to convince them that Japan will continue to be a country that rejects the use of war as an instrument of national policy.

On the other hand, the U.S. and England had their own obligations as winners. Having fought against militarism, they could not very well oppose the yearnings for independence of Asian nations that wanted to be free of Western

• *Explosion of A-bomb on Hiroshima.*

influence. The old imperialism of Western nations, which had gained them large interests and many privileges in China and other Asian nations, started to erode. World War II, particularly the Pacific war, caused the real end of imperialism in Asia.

• *Japanese plenipotentiary team to surrender on the U.S. battleship Missouri.*

Chapter VII: The Era of Global Partnership
33. OCCUPATION AND REFORM

The Occupation of Japan was carried out under the leadership of General Douglas MacArthur, who was appointed as the Supreme Commander of the Allied Powers (SCAP). SCAP conveyed orders to the Japanese government through General Headquarters (GHQ).

The first task of the Allied Powers was to hold war crimes trials to prosecute war criminals. The International Court was opened in May 1946 and war criminals, including former Prime Minister Tojo Hideki and seventeen other defendants, were prosecuted. Similar courts were held both inside and outside Japan, and in all 937 defendants were sentenced to death. The emperor, however, was neither tried nor sent to prison, because SCAP felt he could play an important role in unifying the Japanese public.

Next, SCAP set about making Japan a democratic nation. Over two hundred thousand bureaucrats who had cooperated in war activities were purged from public office. The old constitution was scrapped and a new one was promulgated in May 1947. Under the new constitution, the emperor was redefined as the symbol of the nation instead of as a divinity. Also, Article IX stated that Japan would never again use military force to solve international issues.

Reflecting democratic ideals, the new constitution provided for parliamentary democracy—including universal suffrage for all eligible citizens, men and women. Among the many other reforms, basic democratic freedoms such as freedom of speech, assembly, and union activity, were ensured. Since the *zaibatsu* were a major factor in the Japanese invasion of Asia, GHQ ordered them dismantled. The agricultural system was

• *General Douglas MacArthur arrived at Atsugi naval air base.*

• *Emperor Showa.*

also changed, with tenants now able to own their land.

The war was so devastating that thousands of people lost houses and jobs. Food was in short supply and many urban citizens starved. With union activity and freedom of speech guaranteed, strikes and demonstrations occurred frequently. This caused SCAP and GHQ to see communism as a potential threat.

In fact, the world political situation was already moving quickly toward the cold war era, and the U.S. strongly favored keeping Japan at the strategic forefront of democratic countries in East Asia.

Accordingly, U.S. Occupation policy gradually shifted. While maintaining the goals of making Japan democratic and capitalist, the U.S. now also wanted an independent country with military and economic power strong enough to serve as a buffer against the communist systems in the Soviet Union and China and to protect open markets in East Asia.

To achieve that goal, several American specialists were dispatched to help implement changes in the Japanese tax and business systems. At the same time, Japan's rearmament was initiated. The new Japanese military was called *Jieitai*, or the Self-Defense Forces. Whether such an organization is allowable under Japan's constitution is still a controversial issue.

Based on this revised Japan policy, the San Francisco Peace Treaty was concluded in 1951 with fifty-two allied nations. Simultaneously, *Ampo Joyaku*, or the U.S.–Japan Mutual Security Treaty, was signed, with Japan approving U.S. military presence in its territory. Then Japan applied to join the United Nations and was approved.

Thus, the Occupation officially ended, except for Okinawa and the Ogasawara Islands. In places like Okinawa, where most U.S. military bases were located, people have at times protested against the American presence as an obstacle to having peace and fulfilling local needs. The Ogasawara chain was returned to Japan in 1968, and Okinawa's occupation status finally ended in 1971 when it reverted to Japan's control. The postwar era had finally come to an end.

34. ERA OF HIGH ECONOMIC GROWTH AND THE BUBBLE ECONOMY

Devastated by World War II, Japan needed strong leadership to get back on its feet. Initially, MacArthur filled that need. However, it was the Japanese government and bureaucrats who eventually galvanized the economy and drove it forward. Since the Meiji Restoration in 1868, bureaucrats had always been the real power holders in the Japanese government.

Japan's economic recovery, triggered initially by the Korean War (1950–53), developed rapidly in the 1960s. After Prime Minister Ikeda Hayato promised that

• *Prime Minister Ikeda Hayato.*

Japanese income would double within a decade, the economy took off like a rocket and the annual GDP growth rate exceeded 10%. Per capita income actually tripled in the decade of the 1960s. The symbolic events representing this amazing economic recovery were the Tokyo Olympic Games in 1964—the first Olympics held in Asia—and the inauguration in the same year of the *Shinkansen*, the famous Bullet Train.

But such rapid growth exacted a price, with escalating pollution and vast increases in the cost of goods and real estate. The standard of living simply could not catch up. Improvement in housing standards remains one of Japan's most serious problems, particularly in big cities.

Economic success, however, gradually restored Japanese confidence and, by the 1970s, stimulated Japan to become increasingly involved in international affairs. In the 1980s, Japan became the world's number two economic power and number one in foreign aid. However, it was often accused by key trading partners in the West of enjoying a trade surplus because of unfair trading practices.

Now, after years of economic success, it is questionable whether Japan still needs such a strongly entrenched bureaucracy. On the issue of trade regulations, it was necessary to control the Japanese economy when it was so devastated after the war. Once the world entered the era of free economic exchange, however, many of the old regulations became outdated. Bureaucrats have been resistant to changing their own poli-

• *Opening ceremony of the Tokyo Olympic Games.*

cies, because that would mean a reduction of their power and prestige for having originated those policies in the first place. Both domestic and international pressure for deregulation has intensified.

In fact, Japan has been urged to share the responsibility of being a global partner. This has been a hot item of public discussion in Japan. Since the time of Prime Minister Nakasone Yasuhiro, for example, one of the most important public issues has been whether Japan should give any kind of military aid to the U.N. peace-keeping forces in the world's unstable areas.

By the late 1980s, the strong growth of the Japanese economy spawned the term "bubble economy." The value of real estate escalated precipitously. Financial institutions received huge benefits and stimulated industry to invest. Japanese organizations expanded their offices and factories world-wide.

Unfortunately, this economic inflation caused considerable corruption and created a feeling of distrust toward politicians and bureaucrats. When the bubble burst in 1991 because of the devaluation in real estate, the economy slid into a severe recession that endured throughout the 1990s. The public's approval rating of the government and bureaucracy went downhill along with the economy.

• *Opening ceremony of the Shinkansen.*

35. PREDICTIONS FOR THE FUTURE

The decade of the 1990s may be seen as a turning point for Japan. The tough times caused by the bubble bursting have had not only economic repercussions but social ones as well, causing Japan to face the necessity of change in many of its traditional social values and practices.

Although weakened financial institutions and big industry needed drastic internal change to participate successfully in the new global competition, the entrenched human resource systems and relationships between business and government bureaucrats have remained in place.

As a result, winners and losers emerged. Companies that could not or would not change declined or went bankrupt. Foreign institutions took advantage of the increasing deregulation and the devaluation of real estate to invest in the Japanese market. Japan has thus entered the era of economic diversity.

A change of generations is also taking place. The younger generations that have grown up after the disaster of World War II have begun to put more value on their private lives and leisure time than on the so-called "working hard for the company" mentality that is commonly believed to have created the Japanese economic juggernaut.

This kind of value change also brought on a new controversy about changing the Japanese educational system to foster greater respect for individuality and to prepare Japanese young people to function globally.

Considering Japan's long history, including the Meiji era reforms, these are not easy challenges. Indeed, for Japan as an Asian country, those challenges are made the more difficult with the question of how to incorporate globalizing changes into their traditional Asian values.

In the terrible experience of World War II, Japan learned that risk was fatal if they ignored the

value of synergistic relations between Eastern and Western cultures. That risk was the fascism and militarism that developed as the result of an unbalanced complex between Eastern and Western values that was already planted inside the Japanese mind.

Now the world has come to Japan. And Japan has already begun to mingle in the world but needs to globalize even more. After the cold war ended, the world became more and more diverse. How Japanese handle this new trend is the crucial link to the future. To make the right prediction is not easy.

INDEX

INDEX

INDEX